Sell Your
Crafts on eBay

More than 200 Tactics, Tips and
Tricks to Profit with Your Art and
Craft Items from eBay's Millions
of Buyers Every Day

by
James Dillehay

More books by this author:
The Basic Guide to Pricing Your Craftwork
The Basic Guide to Selling Arts and Crafts
Overcoming the 7 Devils That Ruin Success
Your Guide to Ebook Publishing Success
Guerrilla Marketing for Artists and Craftspeople

Sell Your Craft Items on eBay
ISBN: 0-9710684-5-3

Published by: Warm Snow Publishers
P.O. Box 75, Torreon, NM 87061 **www.craftmarketer.com**

eBay is a registered trademark and a property of its owner.

The statistics and prices provided in this book were gathered from analysis of eBay's sales during 2003 and 2004. The author and publisher provides no guarantee that your auctions will complete at the average prices shown in our examples or at any other prices. The eBay marketplace is in constant flux. We are providing this information solely for the purpose of helping you evaluate the potential for selling your items.

Contents

Acknowledgements

The author and publisher gratefully acknowledge the following people for contributing their wisdom and support.

Roger C. Parker, thank you for providing guidelines for creating One Page Newsletters that auction sellers can use to stay in touch with their customers. www.onepagenewsletters.com

Dr. Joe Vitale, many thanks for your Hypnotic Marketing examples that make seller's auction descriptions compelling to bidders. www.mrfire.com

J.D.

Introduction

Artists, craftspeople and photographers are successfully selling their items on eBay every day. According to a recent analysis of eBay sales, a craft item sells every 9 seconds.

At the same time, many would-be sellers are listing their pieces for sale on auctions and getting no bids, concluding eBay just doesn't work.

Part of the problem is all the hype about people making fortunes selling through online auctions. If someone just starting on eBay has unrealistic expectations of making fast bucks, they can be quickly disappointed.

What we don't hear enough of is how seriously you must take selling on eBay as a business in order to reap real profits.

I'm about to show you step-by-step how to know if your art or craft items will sell on eBay, how to learn what buyers will pay, whether you will make a profit, how to take advantage of a number of factors which constantly influence auction sales, and a host of auction selling success tactics which specifically help artists and craftspeople.

Anyone who can type and has a credit card can put up an auction on eBay. In fact, if you browse through some of the listings for art, craft and photography items, you'll see that many auction sellers have given no time to research, nor thought to creating a compelling auction description. This book gives you scores of tactics for wording your auction titles and descriptions to bring more bidders.

Many artists and craftspeople selling online are using eBay to boost their total overall sales by 10% to 20%. Those who have followed the steps outlined in this report are selling full time on eBay and happily working from home.

Important keys to higher profits are to focus on collecting customer contact information and to follow up with customers regularly to develop a group of loyal collectors. One of the great things buyers love about eBay is getting to interact directly with a craft artist.

Compared to lugging your items around the country displaying at weekend art and craft shows, selling on eBay offers the luxury of working from the comfort of your home. Your audience is 6 million people who visit eBay to shop 24 hours each day from all over the globe.

This guide is in no way meant to suggest or recommend you stop everything else you are doing to market your pieces now and switch over to selling on eBay. If you follow the steps outlined here for researching the market for your work, you'll quickly learn whether selling on eBay is right for your items.

Don't be surprised that if within the course of your study, you discover scores of opportunities for profits only distantly related to selling your own created products. My own research revealed a startling number of overlooked ways to make extra money. The challenge with eBay lies not in a lack of opportunities, but rather in deciding which ones to pursue.

Chapter 1
Art and Craft Items
That Sell on eBay

So many different types of art and craft items are selling every day on eBay, it is impossible to list them all. There are over 150,000 craft items for sale on eBay right now. Sales of craft items on eBay have grown almost 60% in the past year.

In 2003, more than $38 million in crafts and needlecrafts supplies sold on eBay. More than $190 million in photography related items also sold that year. However, these categories are just a fragment of the total value of all items sold in 2003 on eBay, around $20 billion.

As of April, 2004, eBay had more than 104 million buyers and sellers registered; 41,000 of whom are craft sellers listing items through auctions.

To give you a bigger picture of the demand for art and craft items, here are stats for bids and sales on eBay from 2003 and 2004.

• a craft item sold every 9 seconds (about 9,600 per day, over 90,000 each week)
• a scrapbook item sold every minute (about 1,440 per day)
• more than 48,000 bids were placed every day for artwork and antiques
• more than 7,000 pieces of gold jewelry sold every week
• more than 30,000 clothing and accessory items sold every day
• almost 24,000 toys and games sold every day
• 40 cross-stitch items sell in an hour on average on eBay

- on average over 280 art supplies sell daily on eBay
- 5 sewing machines sell on average every hour on eBay

During the months before the Christmas holidays:
- more than 3,000 Christmas items sold every day

Many of the reported sales refer to art and craft supplies as well as handcrafted items. The demand for such supplies on eBay is an opportunity for extra income you should not ignore. See Chapter 12, **More Income Streams From eBay.**

What eBay says about craft sales . . .

> Crafts is one of eBay's fastest growing categories. You can sell as much or as little product as you want and expose your items to an audience of 75 million potential customers. Whether you are selling a single scrapbook or looking to launch your new product line, eBay is a great way to sell your craft items.

Another consideration in placing your work for sale on eBay as well as on other Web sites is that continued branding of your name will contribute to future sales. Branding is often overlooked as a marketing tactic by artists who feel driven to focus on making immediate sales. The important point to remember is that familiarity inspires confidence and confidence is the number one reason people make a purchase.

The artist or craftsperson intent on building a successful career will incorporate strategies that help brand their name among buyers of art and craft items at every opportunity.

Who buys online

Statistics show tremendous growth in online spending with projections of increased numbers for the foreseeable future. The U.S. Commerce Department showed an increase of 25% on ecommerce sales over last year.

One research company predicts that online sales of gifts will increase by a compound annual growth rate of 41 percent during the next five years as more consumers go online to search for gift ideas and presents. As you already know, art and craft make unique gifts sure to be remembered.

According to the *Wall Street Journal*, the average online shopper is 48 yrs old and predominantly female (57%), with an average household income of $52,300. Best of all she spends about $276 online in a 3-month period.

It may also help to learn about the average Internet user. Another survey showed the average user is probably:

- around 41 years old, educated and earning about $65,000 a year
- roughly 50% or more are female
- 47% are married
- 75% of searchers surf intending to buy
- 33% of searchers made a purchase online most of the time

The above statistics show that the average person who surfs the Internet has the disposable income and the inclination to buy online. To find more data on what types of products consumers are buying online see:

ecommerce.vanderbilt.edu/papers.html
www.clickz.com/stats/
www.census.gov (useful for offline sales)

Another productive way to research sales of any product is to search for "statistics product sales" (substituting product for your item) at Google.

Chapter 2
How to Get Statistics
on Craft Sales

By now, you are probably excited and anxious to begin selling your pieces online while working from home in your pajamas. Before you rush over to eBay.com and start putting up auctions, please stop right now and get ready to do a reality check.

The fastest way to lose money on eBay and get discouraged is to put up auctions without first researching whether items like yours are selling. You may feel that everyone just has to love your handmade items. But the truth is your pieces are competing against hundreds and thousands of other listings.

Enjoying a successful eBay business is part science, part creativity. The science part is the research. The creativity develops with time and experience.

I am going to outline steps you should take before you put up your first auction. If you choose not to follow these guidelines, prepare to be disappointed in your online auction results. Before you start placing auctions, you must know:

- what is selling on eBay in your genre — is there a demand?
- how much people are willing to pay for items like yours
- how buying cycles affect sales

The eBay marketplace comprises a dynamic and fluid current of over 104,000,000 users who create the market.

Which items move through the eBay system shifts daily so it is vital that you understand these changes and how to take advantage of these shifts. The solution to navigating and profiting from the eBay market flux is research .... research .... research!

You can only sell items if there is a demand for those items. If no one wants what you are selling on eBay, you won't make any sales there. However, just because an item will not sell on eBay, that doesn't mean it will not sell through other markets like craft fairs, mail order catalogs, stores, galleries or other venues.

You will only get as much money for your items as people are willing to pay for them. This is called the average market value. This book will show you how you can learn, in a few minutes or less, just what the average market value is for any art or craft item you wish to sell on eBay and then determine if it is profitable for you to list your items.

The information here is not meant to encourage or discourage you from placing auctions on eBay. You should only make the decision to list auctions based on what you learn from doing preliminary market research. The research will give you the data you need to make an informed decision.

> Note: If you are brand new to eBay, go and explore the site before reading further. It will help you to be familiar with auctions on eBay, often referred to here as listings. Each auction listing has a 'title', which shows up in a list of search results after typing in words at eBay's search box. When you click on an auction title, you are taken to the auction's 'description', which displays product details and seller terms along with one or more product images.

Research step 1

Go to eBay.com. In the search box, type in the word or phrase that describes your art or craft item. For an example, I typed in "handmade jewelry" and was shown over 150 live auctions.

Research step 2

Next, you find yourself on the results page of auctions for "handmade jewelry". Scroll down the links on the left hand side of the page and click on the link for "Completed items".

When I clicked on "Completed items" for "handmade jewelry", I was shown 300 + completed auctions. So far, so good. I now have a snapshot of how popular handmade jewelry items are. I can see there is a demand for this type of product.

When you run the same search, your results will differ because listings are in constant flux of being added and completing. I recommend you do searches for your items every two to three weeks and take notes of your results. Noting your search results allows you to chart the cycles and record any obvious buying patterns. For the most part, you'll sell more when a buying cycle is peaking and less when the cycle is waning. But if you plan on profiting from eBay over the long term, your recording of buying patterns will help you predict when is the best times to list auctions in future months.

Research step 3

I need to know how much people are willing to pay for my "handmade jewelry" to learn if it is profitable for me to even consider listing my pieces on eBay. If I cannot make and sell handmade jewelry for a profit, this isn't my marketplace.

eBay allows you to sort the completed auction listings by price. Just click on the link that says "highest price". Now your list of completed auctions will be ordered by highest priced items first, descending to the lowest prices. If the list shows lowest prices first, just click on "highest price" again and the sort order will reverse.

You will notice not all completed auctions got bids. For the purposes of our research, you are only interested in the prices of completed auctions, especially the highest priced listings. You want to know what people are willing to pay for items like yours.

Research step 4

Based on the prices your research reveals, decide if you can profitably sell your own art or craft items on eBay. Don't try to fool yourself with wishful thinking. Do the math and determine exactly how much time/labor and cost of materials goes into your item. If it takes you 8 hours to make a piece of jewelry and the highest price similar items sell on eBay for is only $26, you are not going to make a profit. Here's a quick formula for determining profitability:

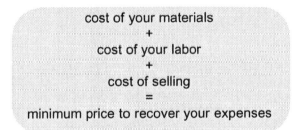

cost of your materials
+
cost of your labor
+
cost of selling
=
minimum price to recover your expenses

I recommend you estimate your own labor costs around a minimum of $10 per hour. If you hire others to produce items, add about 30% of each employee's hourly rate to the total employee payout to account for Social Security, Workman's Comp and added bookkeeping costs.

If your research reveals you cannot sell your items on eBay and make a profit, this does not mean your items would not sell elsewhere for a higher price. For now, we're only examining your prospects for selling on eBay. For finding more markets to sell your work through, see www.craftmarketer.com/selling-crafts.htm

To get more help on strategically pricing your art and craftwork for maximum profits, see www.craftmarketer.com/pricing-crafts.htm.

Research step 5

Up until now, the first 4 research steps can be done at eBay in a few minutes. But you can dig much deeper by accessing analytical tools like those at www.andale.com or by using the software tools described at the end of this chapter.

If your previous research steps show you can profitably sell your craft item on eBay, the next step is to carefully examine and take notes on winning auctions to see how the sellers constructed their auction pages.

Now it's time to use Andale.com or one of the softwares described at the end of this chapter. For this example, I typed in "stained glass" and was shown 2,026 auctions completed at an average closing price of $51.22. Based on analysis of completed auctions, the tools suggest that:

> *Best category to list in would be:*
> Antiques > Architectural & Garden > Stained Glass
>
> *The best starting price would be:*
> Between $0.00 and $13.85 opening bid and
> Between $0.00 and $13.85 reserve
>
> *Best starting time and duration:*
> List on Thursday, between 12noon to 4 pm and
> choose 5 day auction
>
> *Which optional upgrade features to use:*
> Gallery Featured

Analysis then shows how these auctions were diagnosed and lists the auctions included in the analysis. This allows me to examine each of the top winning auctions to see if the items selling are similar to what I want to sell and to explore ideas for potential products.

Here is how to look at the elements successful sellers use to decide if you should include them on your pages:

• Examine the winning auction titles. Pay attention to how successful sellers include keywords in their auction titles.

- Observe how much detail they provide when describing their item.
- Be aware of the style of language sellers use to 'sell' the objects.
- Note the categories under which winning auctions are listed.
- Check whether the seller used any of eBay's special features — bold, featured listing, gallery photos and other ways of enhancing your auction cost extra beyond eBay's auction listing fees.
- Evaluate the starting price, the starting day of the week and the duration of winning auctions.
- Note observable trends of winning auctions. Art and craft items go through cycles of interest on eBay. The time of day, the day of the week, the week of the month and the month of the year all influence sales.

Do not copy other auction listings, images or produce copies of other artist's works. Copying others work without permission is illegal. See page 28 for what to do if you think someone has stolen your content, images or designs.

The purpose behind studying successful auctions is to quickly and effectively learn what customers buy, how much they will pay, and how successful art and craft sellers create winning auctions.

There is no jurying process on eBay similar to art and craft shows. Anyone can list anything that doesn't violate eBay's policies.

With a craft fair, you can only guess about how much you'll sell. Once you apply to a show and are accepted, *"you pays your money and you takes your chances."* With eBay, you can do the research first before you pay.

More research will uncover other opportunities. For instance, you can quickly learn the top selling items that fall under eBay's categories like art, craft, collectibles, pottery, jewelry and more. Not only can you discover what individual items are selling in each category, you can learn what percentage of auctions complete successfully for each category.

Below are examples of specific words and phrases describing auction items researched at Andale.com. All of these numbers come from auctions on eBay completed within a thirty-day period in 2004. When you research these exact search terms yourself, expect to get different results because auctions and listings are constantly changing.

Note that the average selling prices in the list below are derived from adding all the completed auction winning bids and dividing by the number of auctions. There can be a wide range of prices spread throughout the auctions, which you will see when you begin your own research process.

Item Search Term	# Auctions Listed	# Auctions Sold	Average Sell Price
art	90,611	16,269	$37.43
art glass	8,808	3,764	$54.12
art pottery	3,589	1,670	$44.35
art print	46,515	6,435	$15.50
beaded	5,447	1,914	$48.36
birdhouse	20,711	1,585	$9.71
bracelet	172,078	51,176	$38.31
candles	131,093	21,346	$9.89
christmas ornament	14,342	4,128	$18.38
collectible	3,074	1,085	$11.38
craft	134,264	6,559	$7.30
crafting	952	324	$6.20
crochet patterns	10,242	5,272	$5.60
decorative collectible	200	65	$12.81
dolls	114,343	42,874	$21.96
dollhouse	7,372	3,734	$18.81
dragon	31,760	7,764	$17.25
dragon art	797	182	$16.96
dragon pottery	182	51	$30.12
dried flowers	1,064	403	$11.87
earrings	475,390	55,065	$35.07
fairy	10,317	2,757	$30.51
folk art	8,435	3,158	$40.54
gargoyle	5,097	606	$23.58
handbag	31,438	12,517	$50.72
hand crafted	980	242	$22.95
handcrafted	2,839	526	$23.04
handcrafted glass	128	56	$13.70

handmade	2,233	937	$16.29
hand made	1,358	520	$27.81
handmade glass	1,040	472	$16.14
handwoven	206	105	$43.04
jewelry	52,256	17,275	$21.01
jewelry box	17,982	5,640	$25.40
lizard art	140	52	$21.83
maine art	262	59	$35.61
mermaid	4,203	1,102	$19.05
photo frames	16,570	2,944	$9.62
photography	5,225	1,913	$15.65
photography contemporary	27	7	$44.22
pillow	61,288	17,236	$18.06
quilt	44,750	21,018	$43.25
sculpture	18,450	3,080	$85.57
sewing	9,989	3,299	$25.34
shawl	35,651	6,319	$22.76
stained glass	9,579	2,026	$51.22
tapestry	7,427	2,448	$41.53
teddy bear	2,193	613	$20.32
unicorn	12,307	1,620	$19.17
wall decor	5,429	1,705	$12.25
wall hanging	8,855	3,103	$23.29
wind chime	12,777	1,023	$15.27
wood carving	2,081	833	$26.66
wood box	4,040	1,366	$20.12
wood sculpture	728	170	$64.63
wood toy	2,193	613	$20.32
woven	2,723	993	$19.76

The results above include auction items which may be collector's items within a given category. In some auctions, I found collectible items selling for hundreds of dollars while the average selling prices were much lower. Do not assume these numbers guarantee your items will sell for an equal dollar amount or at all. The above research was gathered using Andale.com tools: *Price Finder* (around $4 per month) and *How to Sell* (also around $4 per month)

eBay provides a market for collector items you typically don't find for sale at art and craft shows. In a recent 30-day period on eBay, 11 auctions sold with the words "assembled scale model" in the auction title. The average selling price was $91.33 and the highest priced item, a collector's item, went for $749.

The statistical analysis provided here is to give you an idea of what you can learn through studying eBay auctions, not to encourage or discourage you to make a business decision. Do your own research first before posting auctions.

Research tools

The statistics cited in this report came from studying successful eBay auctions. You can conduct and record similar auction results studies, item by item on eBay, but the hours involved are prohibitive. You will accomplish much more, much faster by using software or services which analyze eBay sales and deliver reports in seconds.

eBay offers several research tools at it's *Seller Central* area. For identifying hot selling items in various categories, see eBay's *What's Hot*, free at <u>http://pages.ebay.com/</u> <u>sellercentral/whatshot.html</u>

At the same link just mentioned, eBay also serves up a *Merchandising Calendar* of what categories will get special promotional attention in the coming months. This feature allows sellers to coordinate purchases with eBay's upcoming promotions.

Outside of eBay, there are highly effective research tools like <u>Andale.com</u>. Andale gives you a menu of tools to choose from, each for which they charge a small monthly fee.

Although eBay offers a *What's Hot* tool, you can also identify market opportunities with Andale's module, also called *What's Hot.* For around $4 per month, you can learn the hottest selling items on eBay for each category and subcategory. You also get analysis on which upgrade elements the winning auction sellers used.

Another Andale.com module called *How to Price* lets you analyze sales by price. For instance, if you type in 'wood sculpture', you'll quickly learn how many auctions with 'wood sculpture' in the title completed successfully, the price range of the listings, and the average closing price. Cost to access *How to Price* is around $4 per month for unlimited use. Andale's *How to Sell* module tells you the statistically best category to list your item under, the best starting time /

day of the week, how long to run the auction, which add-on features to use, and the price range of closing auctions.

You can also purchase software programs like *Deep Analysis* or *WhizAnalysis* which analyze any art or craft market sector on eBay and produce detailed market research reports. These programs can also analyze a particular craft item to see how much it might sell for, and find the best techniques for selling it. You can also see which craft sellers are really doing well, and analyze their techniques and product line. These programs help you learn which categories would be best for your craft items by viewing bid data, sell-through rates, and average sales. For a free 30-day trial, go to www.craftmarketer.com/ebay_auction_software_tools.htm .

Chapter 3
7 Things You Must Know
That eBay Doesn't Tell You

12 Ways to locate sources

Profitability from eBay auctions will come from consistent application of the principle, ***buy low and sell high***. Find sources of products at the lowest possible prices and then sell those items at top dollar.

Art and craft items you make yourself are usually cheaper to produce than buying already made items. But don't hesitate to do the research steps outlined in this guide to learn if you can increase your profits selling other items in addition to those you make yourself.

Regardless of your craft media, there is more than one supplier for your raw materials. Here are 12 ways to locate sources of art and craft items at wholesale or bargain prices.

• One of eBay's categories is "Wholesale" where one can browse through products in mixed lots. Mixed lots may be offered by eBay Power Sellers who have located a low-cost, bulk purchasing deal, manufacturers and distributors with large excess inventory, and individuals just looking to clear out their excess stuff.

Pay scrupulous attention to mixed lot auction descriptions. Make sure you know exactly the items on which you are bidding. Many mixed lot offers will not break down into profitable single item sales.

• Smart eBay sellers scour auction listings that are poorly designed and have few or zero bids. They pick up real bargains this way and then, put up a more enticing listing and sell the items for profit.

- Andale.com provides a *Suppliers* listing where you can list items you are seeking and get matched to wholesale suppliers for those items. To use, go to Andale.com and click on the link for *Suppliers*. Select by category. The *Suppliers* module is free to list on, but costs $3.95 per month for unlimited contacts.

- Buy direct from manufacturers if you are willing to purchase in larger lots. You can always sell the excess on eBay. See Chapter 12, **More Income Streams From eBay** for how to sell craft supplies through auctions. Search for manufacturers of any materials by browsing the Thomas Register, online at www.thomasregister.com, or usually available in your public library's resource section.

- Business closings such as a craft supply store going out of business will provide an opportunity for what is often known as a distress sale. The owner of a failing business is often under pressure to liquidate inventory at prices lower than wholesale. Find notices of business closings through newspaper announcements and looking out for "Going out of business" signs.

- Estate sales occur upon the death of someone whose family seeks to sell personal items rather than keep them. Estate sales are often announced in classified ads.

- Garage sales offer another source of buying items cheaply. You see notices for garage sales almost every weekend.

- Flea markets typically feature tables and tables of odd items, often sold at low prices.

- Local auctions are usually held weekly for a huge variety of merchandise. You can sometimes find lots of items which can be sold individually for profit on eBay.

- Wholesale trade shows may be expensive to travel to, but display hundreds of booths from a wide variety of distributors and manufacturers. To locate trade shows around the U.S., see www.merchandisegroup.com and www.tradeshowweek.com.

- Locate wholesale suppliers for a huge variety of products through the *Directory of Drop Ship Sources* at www.craftmarketer.com/ebay_auction_software_tools.htm.
- Another method of scouting for sources that gets mixed results but is fairly fast is to search for wholesale suppliers from Google.com or Yahoo.com. For example, type in "wholesale craft supplies" and you'll see lots of sites to visit. The challenge with this method lies in sorting true wholesale suppliers from pretenders out to capture unsuspecting bargain hunters. This method will also bring up wholesale source directories for sale, but most of these will be lists of companies you can probably find from your own research.

> Note that most legitimate wholesalers and distributors won't sell direct to the public and require buyers to have a resale certificate, which is the same as a state sales tax permit. If you don't have a state sales tax permit, contact your state's office of taxation and revenue.

Also, try asking other sellers on eBay's forums. But don't expect Power Sellers to reveal their best sources since doing so would be counter productive to their own success.

Multiple uses for a search term

Some of the terms included in example analysis of eBay sales in this guide will encompass a wider array of items than hand made art or craft items. For instance, auctions with the word 'sewing' will include sewing machines and sewing accessories. Craft listings include crafting supplies, crafting tools and equipment.

The more exact your use of keyword terms in your auction titles and descriptions, the easier it will be for browsers to identify auctions with your items. The same rule holds true for when you are researching items like yours to analyze top selling auctions.

Be careful not to assume that the sales statistics and recommendations apply unless you know for certain the auction results you are examining are for items like the ones you want to sell.

At the same time, be aware that your research may uncover additional opportunities. You will discover hot selling items for which you can find sources and turn for a quick profit by selling them on eBay, even though they may have little to do with your craftwork. Hey, it beats working a job.

Popular products with niche names

Another element to consider when researching top selling auctions is the confusion that arises from some popular auction items having similar names to art or craft themes, but then turn out to be completely unrelated.

For instance, the word 'dragon' will appear in listings for all kinds of games and software such as *Dungeons and Dragons* as well as art objects with a dragon theme. Research results will display more listings for 'dragon' than 'dragon art' auctions.

When you want to research theme-related art and craft objects, be sure to include words that narrow the search results to exactly the type of items you are selling, like 'dragon art'.

Style and themes

If your art is theme oriented, and that's always good for marketing your work, you can research auctions by your niche or genre. In other words, you can examine the demand for 'cat' auctions as well as 'cat painting.' This approach can open many overlooked opportunities for sales.

In the sample statistics previously listed on page 18, I included popular items which people collect, like unicorns, teddy bears, gargoyles and others. Note that I often used the singular form of the word, because most auctions are for single items.

If your theme line is bridal crafts, you will be happy to learn that in a recent thirty-day period, 27,757 auctions of wedding items sold on eBay — the top selling item went for $1,350. Among the many types of items sold in these auctions were wedding bands, wedding gowns, wedding plates, wedding bows, and wedding stickers. See any opportunities here?

Timing and seasons

Items geared for holiday sales will usually show more auction listings in the months immediately preceding the date. Examples include Christmas, Easter, Valentine's Day, Graduation Day, Mother's Day, Halloween, and Thanksgiving.

However, don't exclude the possibility of selling nonseasonal items even at other times of the year. You will miss extra sales if you do.

For example, between February 12 and March 12 of 2004, I found 4,107 eBay auctions with 'Christmas ornament' in the title which completed successfully at an average selling price of $17.34. That's great news if you make Christmas ornaments and want more sales year round.

In that same period — and remember this is an off season month — I found 1,793 completed auctions with 'halloween' in the auction titles, with an average selling price of $32.11. For auctions with the word 'thanksgiving', 164 items sold at an average price of $7.91.

Regional interest

If you specialize in art, photography or craft of specific geographical areas, eBay has customers browsing for your regional work. For example, when searching for items from Maine, within a recent 30-days on eBay auctions, there were:

59 'Maine art' auctions closing at an average price of $35.61
106 'Maine photo' auctions closing at an average of $15.86
16 'Maine image' auctions closing at an average of $45.28
79 'Maine coast' auctions closing at an average of $47.89
9 'Maine hand made' auctions closing at an average of $30.94
(search term within single quotes appeared in auction titles)

Spelling of search terms

It is important to consider how people spell the terms for which they search. For instance, 'handmade' (spelled as one word) was found in 2,233 listings in one month with an average closing price of $16.29.

Interestingly, auction titles during that same time which included the spelling 'hand made' (spelled as two words) showed an average closing cost at $27.81, or 58% higher.

Please note, just using the spelling 'hand made' will not alone guarantee you get the same results. You must study and apply all the elements that go into winning auctions. Every edge you can discover from your research should be applied, because analysis of winning auctions reflect the use of the elements we discuss here.

> When doing your research, use the singular form of a word, like mermaid instead of mermaids, because most auctions you want to study will be selling single items. Using the singular form will return more listings to research and those research results will reflect more relevance to your own items. The exception is when you're selling multiple items at a time.

By doing research on winning auctions before you list your own pieces, you can quickly learn what people are willing to pay for each type of item and dissect the important elements which make up a winning listing. You can also capitalize on many elements like timing, spelling of search terms, and regional interest to sell more of your items throughout the year and around the world.

Chapter 4
Copyright, Brand Names, and Keyword Spamming

Copyright your designs

What happens if someone buys one of your pieces and then starts reproducing and selling the same item? If you have registered a copyright for your designs, you have legal grounds to force them to cease. You may even be able to get a financial settlement if you can prove they illegally made money from your designs. Whether you will get enough to cover your legal expenses in pursuing a suit is another matter.

If you are certain that an auction listing on eBay infringes your copyright, trademark, or other intellectual property rights, you can go through eBay's *Verified Rights Owner Program*, VeRO, which helps intellectual property rights owners request the removal of auction listings on eBay that offer items or contain materials that infringe on their rights. This helps protect buyers from purchasing items that may be pirated. See http://pages.ebay.com/help/confidence/programs-vero-ov.html

For more general information on protecting your designs through the copyright law for art and crafts, see www.starvingartistslaw.com.

Protect your images

It's really difficult to keep someone from stealing your images if they are determined to do that. You can try putting your name or logo on top of the product but those can be 'painted' over with a photo program like Photoshop.

JavaScripts can prevent users from 'right-clicking' on an image and saving it to their own computer. Although these scripts might work well for your own Web site, eBay is set up to restrict some JavaScript functions, so they may not work or worse, the JavaScript may keep other parts of the page from functioning.

A clever solution to picture theft is to create an transparent image on top of the real image. When the pirate 'right-clicks', he copies the transparent image, not learning the fact until he pastes onto a page. See http://www.isdntek.com/noclick.htm which provides a free software tool for overlaying pictures with transparency.

Another thing to do is to report image thefts to eBay at http://pages.ebay.com/help/confidence/vero-image-text-theft.html

Comparing your item to brand names

It can happen that your auction listing gets removed because you may have violated eBay's property rights policies without even knowing it. You can avoid problems in advance by familiarizing yourself with the rules at http://pages.ebay.com/help/policies/listing-keywords.html#brand

Rules are tighter for listing titles than for listing descriptions, because more people use eBay's search engine to scan titles. Listing titles are more likely to be abused by sellers.

Refrain from making comparisons between items in a **listing title,** as this is against the rules. Use of words such as "like," "style," and "not" in the title of your listing can easily result in a 'comparison' violation of eBay's search manipulation policy, so avoid using these terms. Examples of 'comparison' violations appearing in listings:

*"Leather Handbag, **like** Louis Vuitton"*
*"Leather Handbag, **not** Louis Vuitton"*
*"Leather Handbag, Louis Vuitton **style**"*

Do not include any brand names or company logos in your listings other than the specific brand name used by the company that manufactured or produced the item you are listing. Certain uses of brand names may also constitute trademark infringement and could expose sellers to legal liability. The following is an example of an item or listing that is not permitted on eBay:

A homemade product that incorporates in its name another company's brand name (such as Beanie™ Box).

In your **listing description** only, you are allowed to compare the item you are offering to one other similar product, so long as your listing is not misleading in any way as to which company made the item offered. Examples:

"This vacuum cleaner does a much better job at cleaning ground-in dirt than Acme brand vacuum cleaners."

"This watch is similar in style to Tag Heuer watches."
        ~ examples from eBay's Keyword Spamming policy

If there are multiple cancellations to your account through violating eBay's policies, they may suspend you.

Keyword spamming

The practice of keyword spamming is using brand names or other inappropriate keywords in an auction title or description for the purpose of gaining attention or diverting users to a listing and are not part of the item's actual description. If your listing is found by eBay to violate the keyword spamming policy, your auction may get canceled

eBay attempts to protect users searching for specific items by curbing attempts of sellers to get more views of their auctions unfairly. For example, a seller is offering an off-brand item and using a major name brand in the listing in order to attract searchers typing in the brand name.

Any words you use in your title and description to describe your item that can be found using eBay's search engine, must be directly related to the item.

For instance, it would be considered keyword spamming to include the following words in an auction description for your art:

> *"oil reproductions, art recreations, gallery, art gallery, impressionist, impressionism, oil paintings, reproduction, painting, recreation, copy, quality, reproductions, recreations, realistic, copies, paintings, old masters, replica, posters, prints, video..."*
> ~ examples from eBay's Keyword Spamming policy

You also have to be careful to avoid using keywords in a listing to refer to your other auctions when those keywords don't apply to the first auction. For example, you cannot include something like *"Please see my other eBay listings for Sponge Bob, collectible Barbies, Rolex watches, and Louis Vuitton bags ."* Instead you would want to include a statement like, *"Please see my other eBay auctions."*

Reporting infringers

You can report sellers who violate any of eBay's property rights policies. Like many issues around copyright and trademark infringement, pirates can get by with something only up until they get caught. When no one reports property rights violations, the infringers flourish off other people's work.

There's another use of reporting violations. Some of those filing complaints about keyword spamming turn out to be sellers using this tactic to remove competitors' auctions.

User agreement

Although somewhat long to read, every seller should go through eBay's User Agreement to understand their responsibilities and liabilities. Access the User Agreement at http://pages.ebay.com/help/policies/user-agreement.html

Chapter 5
What to Expect in
Costs and Income

What auctions cost you

Here are the basic fees you can expect to pay when selling your items on eBay. There are more ways to spend money as a seller than listed here, but these are the typical fees for single auction listings:

• Insertion fee — This is a fee charged to your account when you first list your item on eBay. This usually ranges between $0.30 and $3.30 and is nonrefundable. The insertion fee is based on the starting price for your item and insertion fees vary by the type of listing. For example, here are some insertion fees for auctions:

Starting Price Range	Insertion Fee
$0.01 - $0.99	$0.30
$1.00 - $9.99	$0.35
$10.00 - $24.99	$0.60
$25.00 - $49.99	$1.20

Reserve Price	Auction Fee
$0.01 - $49.99	$1.00
$50.00 - $199.99	$2.00

• Additional option fees — These fees are only charged if you choose optional seller upgrades like: Buy It Now, Gallery, Featured Item, etc. Later in this guide, you'll learn about upgrades. Avoid spending extra money for upgrades until you have learned how to research and evaluate previously completed auctions from which you can learn if it pays for you to include those upgrade features. When research indicates you will win more auctions by adding features, then test some auctions to make sure.

    • Final value fee — This fee is a percentage based upon the final sale price of your item and only applicable if your auction listing closes successfully. In other words, you pay when someone wins the auction.

Closing Value	Final Value Fee
$0 - $25	5.25% of the closing value
$25 - $1,000	5.25% of the initial $25 ($1.31), plus 2.75% of the remaining closing value balance ($25.01 to $1,000)
Over $1,000	5.25% of the initial $25 ($1.31), plus 2.75% of the initial $25 - $1000 ($26.81), plus 1.50% of the remaining closing value balance ($1000.01 - closing value)

    • eBay picture services fees (optional) — eBay offers picture services for working with your images for fees:

Service	Fee
First picture	free
Each additional image	$0.15
Slide show	$0.75
Supersize image	$0.75

eBay's fees are subject to change anytime and there may be other fees depending on the type of auction and your status as a seller. Check their site for all applicable fees.

    • eBay store fee is $9.95 per month. Insertion fees for your eBay store are generally lower from normal auction fees. For a complete list of eBay store fees, see http:// pages.ebay.com/storefronts/pricing.html

Cost of your time

    Once you have completed several auctions, you'll have a sense of how much time it takes you to get your product images, auction titles and descriptions posted as well as how long it takes to pack and ship orders. No matter how quickly setting up auctions can go, you do have to consider the time involved as labor, and therefore, part of your costs. Unfortunately, the IRS will not let you deduct your own labor from your business income if you are a sole proprietor. You can, however, hire your kids or your parents, pay them and deduct wages as a business expense.

Cost of inventory

The area of auction selling which plays the biggest part of how much profit you make is in the cost of your inventory. See Chapter 3 for locating sources of low cost merchandise.

Other expenses

You may also incur costs of packing, shipping and insuring items to customers, unless you clearly state in your auctions that the buyer pays these costs.

Other expenses which will probably arise after you have accumulated some experience in auction selling include purchasing keyword banner ads on eBay (described later), auction management software, postal / shipping scale, hiring of employees, bookkeeping costs, and possibly warehouse rent should your inventory become too large for the house.

How much will you earn

In the beginning of your auction business, any expectations you have about earnings is guesswork. With time, you will get a feel for the eBay art and crafts marketplace and a sense of predictability. Although you can rarely be 100% accurate in forecasting profits, you can reasonably expect to be right 70% to 80% of the time after you've been in the auction game consistently for a couple of months.

It's not just the eBay marketplace you have to get familiar with, you also have to know yourself and have a realistic appraisal of how fast and how much you are willing to work at putting up auctions and fulfilling orders.

Your profits will be determined by how much time, energy and commitment you give to your auction business. If you plan to only sell art and craft items on eBay part-time, your earnings will reflect part-time involvement.

The beauty of selling your items on eBay is that you can grow your auction business step-by-step, month-by-month. If you find yourself enjoying the process, you can turn it into a full-time business. After you get the taste of success, you will most likely find selling on eBay an exciting and fun alternative to working for someone else.

I've read articles posted on Web sites of artists reporting sales of $5,000 to $20,000 of their work on eBay per month. I've also come across stories of people who sold little or nothing.

So the short answer to "how much will you make selling on eBay?" is it depends on how much effort you put into it. How much time are you willing to devote to researching and studying other sellers' successes and measuring your own results?

Another element to remember is that your biggest income stream on eBay isn't derived from making sales. Sales are one-shot hotties that make you jump up and down with glee. But while everyone else is going for sales, you should be looking at building a following of loyal repeat customers.

People buy from those they know and trust — a good reason for getting positive feedback ratings on eBay. Once you make a sale, you have the person's contact info which you should treat like gold. Send out newsletters, announcements of special offers, and teasers about a new product line. See the chapter on follow-up for a host of excuses to stay in touch with your customers.

The successful seller recognizes that the lifetime value of a customer far exceeds the gains from a single sale and does everything she can to build and sustain relationships with customers.

Chapter 6
Auction Basics

Types of auction listings

Here are descriptions of the different types of auction listings you can post at eBay.

Buy It Now - As a seller, you can use this option to set a price you are willing to sell your item to any buyer who is willing to pay that price without going through the bidding process. Auction listings with Buy It Now show up like normal auctions, but feature a Buy It Now price.

Fixed Price - Much like Buy It Now, the Fixed Price format lets you buy or sell items at a set price. Buyers can purchase items immediately without bidding or waiting. As a seller, you can sell items at the price you want without waiting for your listing to end. You can use the Fixed Price listing to sell more than one item at the same time.

Reserve auctions - A reserve price is a specific price that you will absolutely not sell lower than. Bidders are aware there's a reserve price, but they do not have access to what it is unless you mention it in your description. To win the auction, the bidder must have submitted the high bid and must meet or go beyond the reserve price. Typically, when the reserve price is not met, the seller does not make the sale and the highest bidder is not obligated to buy.

I get mixed reports about the success of using reserve auctions. Some sellers say reserve prices do not hamper bids and others say they do. A reserve price is hidden to the bidders and is an amount you predetermine the bidding must meet to win. Some bidders avoid reserve price auctions because they have no idea what the value of the piece is.

Dutch auctions - This type of auction is for selling multiple copies of the same item. An example would be 10 mugs, 17 sets of earrings or 25 pattern books. Sellers list an opening bid or minimum price along with the number of items for sale. Bidders enter the price they want to pay and the quantity to buy. All winning bidders pay the same price— the lowest successful bid.

Private auctions - This kind of auction protects a buyer's privacy. Bidders' email addresses are not displayed on the item or bidding-history screens. When the auction ends, the seller is the only one who knows the winner. Private auctions can't be tracked by the bidder and so, are less popular.

How people find your auction

Customers who shop eBay use different ways to find what they want. The most popular method is typing in words describing the item in eBay's search box. After entering a search term, the visitor is shown a results page with auctions that include the search terms in the auction's title.

Do a search for an item like yours at eBay and sort the completed auctions by highest price as explained in Chapter 2. Notice that you not only find the keywords you typed in the search box included in the auction titles, but also other words used to describe the auction.

The more thought-out and precise your use of keywords, the more customers will find your auction. However, be careful to avoid spamming your auctions by including key-word phrases solely for the purpose of getting more views. This is called keyword spamming and is against eBay's policies, which means they can end your auction and suspend you from selling. See Chapter 4 for examples of keyword spamming and how to avoid getting in trouble.

A searcher can expand the number of search results by checking a small box under the search box that says "in titles & descriptions", which then returns results that include auctions with the keywords in the auction page's text. However, fewer people search within descriptions because they quickly learn they get a huge number of irrelevant results.

Another way of finding items on eBay is to start a search by first clicking on a category and drilling down through the subcategories to browse all listings by topic.

In your auction titles and descriptions, include obvious words that not only describe your item, but are also popular search terms.

For example, if you are listing a tapestry, include words like 'wall hanging', 'art', 'woven' and 'collectible' in your title, as long as they actually apply to the item you are selling.

Each of those words and phrases are popular search terms. Within a recent thirty-day period, the following are search results of auctions with those search terms in the auction titles.

Search Term	# of Auctions
art	90,611
wall hanging	8,855
woven	2,723
collectible	3,074
tapestry	7,427

The more terms, the more times the auction will show up in searches. For example, your auction title could read "Collectible Hand Woven Wall Hanging Tapestry".

However, the words you choose must refer to the specific item and not appear as keyword spamming, that is an attempt to include inappropriate keywords in a title or description for the purpose of gaining attention or diverting users to a listing as described in Chapter 4.

How to choose the best categories

Your choice of category(s) is important in helping your art or craft item sell. After you have researched and identified completed auctions for items as outlined in Chapter 2, note which categories under which winning auctions appeared.

The best category to list a finished handcraft on eBay depends on what the item is. Check out the list below to see where most people are listing their handmade items.

There may eventually be a category specifically for 'handcrafted'. Meanwhile, people search for 'handcrafted' this or 'hand made' that in other categories. It will help your listing show up more often by including those words in your auction title.

You can also list your item in two categories, like Self Representing Artists and Folk Art. When you use two categories, you pay double fees, but you also get twice the exposure.

Categories where handcrafted items are found
Afghans, Throws
Candles & Incense
Clothing & Accessories
Drawings
Equestrian, Fishing, Hunting
Furniture
Home Decor
Musical Instruments
Paintings
Photographs
Pottery & Glass
Quilts & Blankets
Rugs & Carpets

Specific categories for handcrafted items
Artist Bears
Artist Dollhouse Miniatures
Artist Dolls
Artist Jewelry
Folk Art
Handcrafted Arts
Handcrafted Dollhouses
Handmade Lampwork Beads
Handmade Marbles
One of a Kind Barbie Dolls
Personalized, Customized Items
Self Representing Artists
Soaps

eBay updates their categories so monitor them frequently in order to take advantage of improved listing opportunities. You can view all subcategories at eBay's portals to art and craft items at http://art.ebay.com and http://crafts.ebay.com

The best starting price to set for your auction

People come to eBay to get a good deal. They probably won't pay as much as you would get for your handmade piece in a fine gallery, but then again, you don't get paid the full amount from a gallery sale, more like 50% on average.

The best way of setting prices is to do the research based on the steps described in Chapter 2. Research will tell you quickly what people are willing to pay for items like yours. This doesn't mean you should set your starting price at the closing prices of previous successful auctions. If the starting price appears too high, no one will bid.

Closely observe the completed auctions with items similar to yours. Did they get 1 bid, 5 bids, 25 bids or just how many on average? The more bids an item received, the more likely the bidders drove the price up from a low starting bid.

The analysis tools mentioned in Chapter 2 will analyze previous winning auctions and suggest an ideal starting price. See the example on page 16 for 'stained glass' auctions where it was recommended:

The best starting price would be:
Between $0.00 and $13.85 opening bid and
Between $0.00 and $13.85 reserve

You can set the starting bid at any amount you choose, but realize you have to sell the item for the winning bid. If you are worried that you won't get enough money for your item, you can do either of two things.

You can set a starting price such that you can live with that price should only one person bid and win. Unfortunately, if your starting price is too high, no one will bid.

Or an improved scenario: you set up a reserve price auction which means that unless the bidding reaches an amount you predetermine, there will be no winner. The reserve price is hidden from bidders unless you tell them the amount in your description.

An example would be you want to get $100 for a hand-made gold bracelet so you set the reserve price at $100. You can set the starting price at $1, $5 or any amount you choose. Unless a bidder enters $100, the auction will not have completed.

You can also preset prices for items and set up a store on eBay using what is called 'Buy it Now'. Many sellers use 'Buy it Now' (extra charge from eBay) buttons that allow shoppers to bypass the auction process and go straight to a storefront, purchase the item and complete the transaction.

As for analyzing eBay's completed auctions to get average prices for items like yours, average winning bids for art and craft related items will probably differ from hour to hour, day to day and week to week because of the constant flux of items entering and leaving the marketplace.

When an item is related to a celebrity who is getting intense coverage in the media, there will be more bids while the press coverage is running strong.

It is important to note that when there are many auctions for the same or very similar items, the bids will be lower because of the larger supply. During times of larger supply, your auction will experience a lower perceived value. Auction prices will close higher when the supply is limited.

You will often get higher closing bids if you time your auction to begin when there are less auctions running for similar items.

Chapter 7
How to Set Up an
Auction Step-by-Step

It is extremely easy to sell on eBay. Go to eBay.com, look for the box that says "Sell" and click. Then just follow the directions.

eBay simplifies the process of setting up auctions so that anyone who can type, can put up a listing. Browsing through auction listings at random will show this to be true. By paying just a little more attention to your listings than the average seller, you can make your auctions stand out and win more bids.

Here is a suggested set of basic steps, some of which may not be included on eBay's site, but are necessary to help you streamline your set-up process:

Prior to listing an item:

√ Have the item's original retail price. This is important so customers can value shop.

√ Make a list with the size, weight, brand names, quantity and materials.

√ Prepare one or more digital images of the item and save to a file that you can quickly retrieve from when you are ready to list.

√ Choose an auction format: Auction-style, Auction-style with Buy-It-Now, or Fixed Price

√ Choose the length of auction duration (3, 7, 10 days)

√ Determine a starting price or write down a Fixed Price, if any.

√ Set up payment methods: Pay Pal, credit cards, checks, money orders or other.

√ Describe shipping options: (USPS, UPS, Fed Ex, customer pick-up).

When you are ready to list your auction:
√ Log into your eBay seller account.

√ Select a selling format for your auction.

√ Choose your eBay category (or categories). You can choose more than one, but you pay additional final value fees for each category.

√ Add your item title and description. The following chapters provide tactics for writing compelling copy.

√ Write your HTML code. HTML code allows you to use colored text, bold and underlined styles and create tables to help shape your auction's appearance.

√ Upload your images. Your product images are very important, see Chapter 8.

√ Select the type of auction and your terms.

√ State your starting price. Plan your pricing by doing the research outlined earlier in this guide.

√ If your earlier research indicates using optional features to increase bids, add them in. Examples: Gallery, bold, featured.

√ State your payment options and shipping terms.

√ Decide if you will use the optional 'Checkout' function which is supposed to help speed completion of payment when an auction ends. Some sellers, however, report problems with Checkout because it allows winning buyers to send payment before shipping can be calculated. You can disable this option in your eBay preferences.

√ Have items on hand ready to ship or have an arrangement with a manufacturer or supplier to drop-ship orders.

√ Save your auction listing info in a spreadsheet or database file for future use.

√ Submit your auction.

√ You will get a confirmation page or email with a number for each auction you are posting. Write this number down or enter the number in your spreadsheet or software for tracking auctions.

After your auction is listed:
√ Be ready to answer emails from bidders needing more information. Be sure to answer inquiries as soon as you can.

√ When the auction ends successfully, you and the highest bidder will get email notification of the auction's completion. Contact the winning bidder within three days — the sooner the better. Confirm the final cost, including any shipping charges, and tell them where to send payment. When the bidder sends in payment to you, send his item.

√ Give feedback of your buyer. Usually, a buyer will post feedback when you post feedback about him. Be courteous and prompt when communicating with customers to insure you get high feedback ratings.

√ If you need to go back to the details of your auction, the history of your listing remains posted for 30 days.

Now repeat the above process for every auction you list. You can have as many listings up as you can manage. Use a bulk listing tool like the free *Turbo Lister* utility described in Chapter 12.

How to write auction titles that get more viewers

As mentioned earlier, most buyers on eBay shop by using title searches. Your title shows up in a list of search results whenever someone does a search using keywords included in your auction title.

• You only have up to 45 characters to describe your item, so make the most of them. Only include words both specific to your item and popular as search terms.

• Every character in the title is critical to helping users find your items easily. For each item you plan to sell on eBay, you'll need an auction title. Experiment with titles and reuse those which generate successful auctions. For more ideas, research other winning auctions for how the sellers worded their titles.

- Since some users search using broader terms, you may get good results including the item's category in the title, like "stained glass". If you have multiple listings of the same craft item, consider using related terms for some of those listings, like "art glass".

- Other users search for specifics like model numbers, so if you are selling craft tools, equipment or supplies, include important specifications in your listings. Craft supplies may be best described in the title by including brand, material, color or theme, size, weight, or amount.

- Get ideas for more keywords by looking at popularly searched keywords in your category. Do a search on eBay for "your craft item". When the results page shows up, note related terms under 'Popular Searches' shown in the left hand column of eBay's browsing pages.

- If your keywords are often misspelled, it may pay you to include them in your auction titles as you will pick up typo-error prone spellers.

- When composing your auction title, eliminate prepositions like 'with', 'and' and 'that'. Do not include words no one searches for like 'MUST SEE', 'best', 'unique', 'unusual', 'L@@K', 'WOW' or 'greatest'. Also skip the exclamation marks !!!!! and added punctuation like commas and periods.

- Another big mistake is using ALL CAPS thinking that people will notice your auction more. What they notice is that they can't read all caps as well as normal capitalized words so they just skip over those auctions.

- No one searches for punctuation marks and junky come-on words when they are looking for specific items. When you include them in your titles or in your descriptions, you are wasting valuable characters on nonsense text. Make those 45 characters count.

- Avoid attempting to trick browsers by including

keywords of competing products just to show up more often in searches. This is keyword spamming as explained in Chapter 4.

24 elements to include on auction descriptions

In addition to a title, your auction listing will display a description page where you list details about your item and image(s). Like your title, the description page contains keywords that help you show up in searches.

Your auction's description page must convince bidders they have at last found the very thing they have been seeking. They must immediately perceive it as having value or they'll be off bidding on other listings. To insure you grab visitors' attention right away, include the following pieces of information for each item where applicable:

- name of piece
- statement of the piece as an original or reproduction
- brand name
- size / dimensions / weight
- material contents
- media
- installation or assembly required
- care instructions
- framed or unframed, if photos or art
- date of creation
- personal story of what inspired you to make this piece, what went into the making, how long it took — give buyers a way to relate to you as the artisan
- include popular keywords searchers might use to find items like yours, as you did in your auction title; remember not to violate any of the keyword spamming rules.

In addition, there is information to include on all your auctions, which you can create as a text file and simply copy and paste into your new auctions. Repeatable information includes:

- your name as the artist or craftsperson
- 7 word description that makes you stand out
- forms of payment you accept; Pay Pal, credit cards, money orders, etc.
- shipping options: UPS, USPS, FedEx, etc.
- whether you ship C.O.D.
- if buyer pays shipping, packaging and insurance
- if shipping is free, put this in big bold letters
- note for buyers within your state about addition and collection of state sales tax
- return policy and who pays shipping
- damage during shipping claims — most likely covered by insurance
- notice if you ship outside the U.S. and applicable terms and payment in U.S. dollars; include note that buyer is responsible for customs duties for their country
- end with "place your bid now".

Like with auction titles, avoid using hype words, extra punctuation marks !!!!! and ALL CAPS in your description text. Again, remember: ALL CAPS ARE HARD TO READ.

Look and feel of your auctions

In addition to including specific information and images, your auction page will have an overall look and feel. The more professional your auctions appear, the more bids you'll receive.

eBay provides auction page templates that ease the design process of creating pages quickly. Even though they are simplistic, they help get you started. To use their templates, look for *Listing Designer* in the seller guide and note that it comes built into *Turbo Lister*, a free bulk loading utility available for download at http://pages.ebay.com/turbo_lister/

Find more free and low cost auction listing templates by searching for "auction templates" at any major search engine.

Whether you use templates or create your listing from a

blank page at eBay, you can manipulate the HTML coding of your auction pages to include tables, backgrounds, borders, sounds and even include your own shipping calculators. You'll need to be comfortable working with HTML, but these tweaks can add extras to your listings unavailable through eBay. See *eBay Hacks* by David A. Karp for many tips and actual examples of HTML code for how to tweak your auction listing pages.

Payment options

You and your buyers need a way to transfer payment from them to you for winning auctions. The easier it is for customers, the more likely they will bid.

Explain clearly on your auction descriptions exactly what payment options buyers have to choose from. The more popular payment options include Pay Pal (an electronic payment processor at www.paypal.com), credit cards, money-orders and checks.

eBay owns Pay Pal and you can set up your auctions to include a button called 'Pay Now' which takes the winning bidder into Pay Pal for processing payment. However, when you include the 'Pay Now' button, you won't be able to offer other payment options outside of Pay Pal since the buyer goes directly there. Still, some sellers prefer to work only with Pay Pal to speed payments.

If you don't already have a Pay Pal account, get one. It is free and it is essential for doing business on eBay. Pay Pal also offers a free shopping cart for processing sales outside of eBay through your Web site.

Electronic payments are faster and easier. A problem with accepting checks and money-orders for auction payments is that both activities take time and involve several steps the buyer must take. Some of your winning bidders may even forget to send you payment because they put off those steps. On your part, you have to confirm a check is good before shipping the item.

The easier you make it for someone to pay you right away, the faster you'll get your money. Electronic payment through Pay Pal makes it simple for the customer and speeds funds into your account. These services also make it easy for you to keep track of payments because every detail is available to you through your Pay Pal account 24 hours a day online.

If you don't already have a credit card merchant account for accepting Mastercard, Visa, American Express and Discover, you can apply through your Pay Pal account.

Chapter 8
How to Write Compelling Auction Descriptions That Get More Bids

With all the competing auction listings, your auction must stand out and catch each visitor's attention right away.

Imagine there's a way of writing that literally compels more people to bid on your auctions. It's called hypnotic writing and this chapter will help you begin incorporating this strategy on to your auction pages right now for an immediate increase in bids.

Here are 25 hypnotic marketing tactics from Dr. Joe Vitale that you can use to write irresistible and compelling auction descriptions and improve your Web site's conversions of visitors to customers.

Of course, you only want to use these descriptive phrases when they are true about your item.

- Grab people's attention with a good headline:
How To...
Discover...
Imagine...
Attention...
Warning...

- Tell people your item is popular with others"
Best-seller
Very popular
Over (no.) items sold in (no.) days!
People from all over the world have used it
(No.) people have already bought

• Tell people your product is new and in the original package:

100% original
No artificial ingredients
Never opened

• Tell people if the item comes with instructions that are easy to understand:

Clear language
Clearly explained
Clearly written
Easy to understand
Easy to read
Written in everyday language

• Tell people specific and detailed benefits the item provides, like:

By (no.) %...
In (no.) minutes...
Less than a week...

• Tell people you offer help with assembly or care:

Comes with easy-to-follow instructions
Get step-by-step help from me
Care instructions provided

• Tell people item is available for immediate delivery:

I ship your order the same day I receive payment
Available for immediate delivery
I offer an "Overnight Delivery" option

• Tell people what other people have said so that will persuade them to use your item:

I read in a (source) that...
I saw on (source) that...
I heard on (source) that...

- Tell people if your item has been seen on TV or mentioned in the news:
  As seen in (the magazine(s) name)
  As seen on (the TV show)
  As heard on (the radio station)
  As mentioned on (TV, the radio)
  As mentioned on (the Web site)

- Tell people they have plenty of payment options:
  Fastest delivery when you use Pay Pal
  Pay with Mastercard, Visa, American Express, Discovery
  Money Orders accepted

- Tell people the item is 100% tested and proven:
  Time-tested
  Proven effective
  Battle tested
  100% tested and proven

- Tell people they can only get the item from you:
  You won't find this in (location)...
  You won't see this anywhere else

- Tell people to act before the item is gone:
  Bid now or this one-of-a-kind item will be gone forever
  After this auction, there will be no more
  Act now before it's gone

- Tell people when they buy from you, their contact information will be kept confidential:
  Your information is completely confidential
  Your information will never be sold
  Your information will never be seen by any outside organization
  We will never pass your e-mail on to a 3rd party

- Tell people they get something for free when they buy your item:

  Buy it now for ($) and you'll get (gift) for free
  It costs ($) but I'll give you (gift) free if you win the auction

- Tell people the item is collectible:

  Limited edition
  Only selling (no.) of this version
  Add it to your series
  Only ( ) autographed copies left

- Tell people how long you have been in business:

  I've been in business 12 years
  I'm an eBay seller since 1998
  I've been helping people get their craft items for 7 years

- Tell people the positive or negative emotions and feelings they will get from using or not using your item:

  Attractive
  Adored
  Cheerful
  Challenged
  Confident
  Comfortable
  Disappointed
  Embarrassed
  Enthusiastic
  Excited
  Frustrated
  Happy
  Loved
  Passionate
  Secure
  Sympathetic

- Tell people how valuable the item is:

Worth ($)
That totals ($)
A ($) value

- Tell people you both have something in common to persuade them to buy your item:

We both know...
Like you I also...

- Tell people to act:

Place your bid now
Now it's time to bid
Click and bid now, this item won't be around for long

- Give people a vivid description of your content, using plenty of adjectives and words that attract the senses:

Feel
See
Picture
Taste
Hear
Smell
Bright
Loud

- Tell people your personal story, so they can relate to you:

Once upon a time...
Just the other day...
One day...
Way back in (year)...
Last week...
Last year...

• Tell people to imagine what will happen if they use or don't use your item:

Imagine
Visualize
Envision
See yourself
Picture
Think about

• Give people an indirect command that will persuade them to use your item:

You may want to...
Possibly you should...
You may realize you...
Surely you will...
I trust you'll...

The tips in this chapter were excerpted and adapted from *Hypnotic Traffic Tools, 99 Ways to Persuade People to Use Your Hypnotic Traffic Tools,* written by Dr. Joe Vitale and Larry Dotson. For more resources on writing hypnotic copy, see www.mrfire.com/ebooks.html

I applied many of Joe's hypnotic writing tactics to my Web site and auction descriptions and experienced an immediate 30% increase in sales. He is author of several bestselling guides including *Spiritual Marketing.*

Chapter 9
18 Tactics That Make
Your Photos Sell

The photo images you use in your auction listings may be the single most important influence on getting bids. If you are thinking to put up auctions without photos, save your money; people must see a photo to believe there's something real to bid on. Images of your art or craft items shown on your auction are the only thing bidders can actually look at.

The better your images, the more bidders you'll get. Here is a checklist of key tactics to use when creating your product images that will make them sell for you:

• When you are selling 3-dimensional objects, include photos taken from different viewpoints so viewers get a sense of depth. Each view should be looking straight at the object. Angle shots make an item look skewed or damaged.

• Take photos in daylight or under Halogen lights (whiter light) or color-balanced lighting.

• When arranging a product photo shoot, choose soft pastel colors for backgrounds or use solid black.

• Use a plain background to make your item stand out. Don't use a white background as it tends to create too much contrast. Use a drape or a blank wall for your backdrop.

• Do not include other objects or Mother Nature scenes in your image shot background because these clever backgrounds do not sell, they only distract from your item.

• Your image colors should be bright with good contrast between dark and lighter areas.

• Digital images can be cropped, color-balanced, contrasted, and enhanced in many ways using a photo-management software. You can work with your images in a variety of formats suitable for using on the Web and for creating product flyers and brochures. *Photoshop* by Adobe is a popular if pricey photo-management software program. *Paint Shop Pro* is cheaper but without as many features. If you are shopping, the best deals will probably be found on eBay.

• Your eBay auction images must load quickly. Don't use large graphic files because they slow down page loading time. People will not wait. If you need a larger image, create a thumbnail to use on the auction page with a note "click on image for larger picture."

• Resize your image files to 300 pixels tall by 400 pixels wide for your eBay auction pages.

• By taking photos using a digital camera, you can connect your camera to your computer and save the photo to your computer as a .JPG format, which is the preferred format universally used for Web images. Although a good digital camera may seem expensive, the cost of your time saved in converting slides and photos to digital formats will pay for itself if you plan on doing a lot of auctions.

• You can take photos with a regular camera and then scan them with flatbed scanner which allows you to convert the photograph to a .JPG format image. If you are scanning photos, specify a scanning resolution of 300dpi (dots per inch) for good images. You can always resize them later for fast loading. Depending on the dimensions of your scanner, you may be able to place flat objects directly on the scanner's bed to create an image.

• If you have slides, you'll need access to a scanner that specifically works with slides.

• If you choose not to make your digital images with a digital camera or scanner, you can take your photos or slides to most photo-film developing locations and they can create a disc with your digital images ready to transfer to your computer. Ask them to create the images at 300dpi. Check with your film developing service to learn if they use Kodak

PhotoNet, a service which digitally publishes copies of your photo images to the Kodak PhotoNet.com Web site from which you can then copy your images to your computer.

• For previewing your images, set your own monitor at the highest color resolution. But be aware most computer monitors will view colors slightly different. Older monitors show less accurate color resolution. Though there's nothing you can do about your viewer's monitor, you can put a notice on your auction which reminds them colors on their monitor will not show the full colors of the original object.

• You can load images directly to your auction pages, host them on eBay, or host them on other sites. See the list of free image hosting sites at http://www.bulls2.com/indexb/freeservers2.html

• Copying other people's images from Web sites, auctions or print publications may be illegal. Unless you see a notice or have evidence that an image is in the Public Domain, assume that every image you see is copyright protected, because the copyright law says an image owner does not have to display a copyright notice; the copyright is legal when the originator creates the image. See Chapter 4 of this book for what to do if you feel someone has infringed on your copyrights.

• Use eBay's Gallery option to upgrade your listing. Gallery option puts a thumbnail image of your item when auction titles are shown to search inquiries. Although the Gallery option costs you an additional 25 cents, it gives your auction prominence and typically gets more bids. Resize your image to 96 x 96 pixels for Gallery images.

• As mentioned earlier, there's little you can do to protect your images from determined thieves. See page 28 for ideas.

• Get more help with working with images on your auction pages by joining eBay's *Photos & HTML Forum* at http://forums.ebay.com/db2/forum.jsp?forum=99 The page offers a great list of tutorial-like articles on various aspects of lighting, backgrounds, equipment and more.

Chapter 10
Auction Features That
Improve Success

eBay is a dynamic market and therefore constantly in flux. Getting more of your auctions to complete successfully and getting top dollar for your art and craft items can be helped by getting good feedback, selecting the best starting day, including optional features for your listing, using eBay's Keyword program, and becoming a Power Seller.

Get good feedback

eBay provides user feedback ratings for buyers and sellers. Feedback ratings, positive ones that is, are the most important way of conveying trust to the potential customers who don't know you.

When browsing auction listings on eBay, buyers take into consideration your feedback rating before placing a bid.

When a seller has negative feedback, an experienced buyer won't bid. Therefore, it is important that you make it a priority to always follow up with customer inquiries and provide prompt delivery in order to elicit the highest feedback ratings you can. Whenever you have occasion to be in contact with a customer during the fulfillment process, always be courteous and respectful to insure you get the best ratings.

Be aware that when you leave feedback for others, people read your comments and associate them with your user name. If you use negative or hateful language, it will make others be less inclined to do business with you.

You can take measures to prevent bad feedback ratings by anticipating and preparing for situations which may present potential problems. I've found that being friendly and fast to respond to questions results in positive feedback every time.

Here's a checklist of prevention measures you can use with your auction descriptions and in your communications with customers:

√ Be completely honest about your item.

√ Ask bidders to be certain the item is what they want before placing a bid.

√ Be prompt, polite and friendly when responding to even dumb questions, which you will receive by email.

√ Don't lie about your item's condition. If it has been used, be sure to say so.

√ List any defects, scuffs, or scratches, even small ones.

√ If you are selling items made of fabric, let bidders know if they are from a smoke-free and pet-free home.

√ Include exact measurements, weights and other qualifying descriptions of your items.

√ Invite inquiries from bidders who may want additional information and assurances.

√ Put a notice on your listings asking bidders to please read your payment and shipping terms before they place a bid.

√ Specify whether you will ship internationally.

√ Check out a bidder's Feedback Rating. If they have negative feedback, you can tell them politely, you don't deal with users with lower than a certain rating. Also include it on your 'About Me' page and on your auction descriptions.

Auction starting day and duration

The time of day and day of the week you begin your auction and its duration will have an effect on your auction's success. For instance, a seven-day auction has a much better chance of attracting more bidders than a three-day listing.

The analysis tools mentioned in Chapter 2 give you suggestions as to the best days to begin your auctions and how long they should last, based on analyzing successfully completed auctions.

For example, analysis of 1,865 winning auctions with

'birdhouse' as a search term, suggested starting a 'birdhouse' auction on Monday, between 10pm and 8am. Note these suggestions may differ if you do the same analysis because of the dynamic flux of the eBay marketplace.

Your auction should end at a time of day that people will most likely be able to bid on auctions they are following. For example, if you begin an auction at 3am, it will close at 3am, but how many people will you exclude from following the bidding by choosing this time of day?

You will probably discover that with art, craft and photography related items, there will be more cyclical periods of bidding, unlike items such as computer parts which get more consistent bids year round.

Use the tools in Chapter 2 to analyze winning auctions by category and by week or month so that you can assess the cycles occurring in your genre. No buying cycle will recur forever, even though it might go on for months or years.

Remember to treat eBay as a dynamic and growing marketplace that requires frequent assessment and you will achieve higher profits and fewer disappointments.

Optional upgrades for your listing

For various fees, eBay allows you to use additional elements on your auction listing to help it stand out. On the seller's pages, you'll view statistics which may indicate, for instance, using bold increases your bids by 23%. However, they make no guarantees your bolded auctions will get bids.

Be cautious in how you evaluate statistics — eBay's, Andale.com's or any other analytical tool's suggestions. There are many factors that go into successful auctions. Although you won't see it discussed very often, there is a totality of all the individual elements interacting together which influences bids. Most important is the demand factor.

The only way to know for certain if an upgrade is profitable is to test the use of various features and see how they affect your results over time.

The following are popular eBay upgrades. Find more at eBay.com's seller's guide along with prices for each option.

- Buy it Now — adds a button allowing customers to click and purchase the item immediately.
- Gallery — allows you to include a small thumbnail photo image that precedes your title and description when your auction shows up in search results. The Gallery option gives your auction prominence and typically gets more bids.
- Bold — adding bold to the title of your listing will make it stand out, unless all the other listings are also bolded.
- Highlight — emphasizes listing with a colored band in the background that makes it stand out from the other listings.
- Featured on Home Page — Your listing will have a chance to rotate into a special display on eBay's home page. Your item is very likely to show up on the Home page, although eBay does not guarantee that your item will be highlighted in any way.
- Featured Plus — your item will be shown prominently in the Featured Items section of its category list. It will also appear in the regular, non-featured item list. Featured Plus is only available to sellers with Feedback Rating of 10 or more. Featured Plus upgrade is $19.95 per listing. You could use this as a form of brand-name advertising campaign to boost name recognition for you as an artist. The more often people read or hear your name, the more familiar you become to them, bringing them closer and closer to making a purchase or to recommending you to others.

Buy It Now and your own eBay store

When listing items on eBay, you can offer your product at a fixed-price or have buyers compete for the item and let the highest bid determine the final sales price.

The option buyers choose to purchase at a fixed price is a 'Buy It Now' button graphic. About 25% of eBay craft sales are in a Fixed Price format. That is, browsers click on the 'Buy It Now' button to purchase immediately. You don't have to have an eBay store to use 'Buy It Now'. The cost for an eBay store is $9.95 a month. Advantages include:

- establishes credibility and instill customer confidence
- lets you offer items at a variety of prices
- lets you showcase a wide inventory of items
- you can add new pieces quickly
- creates a gallery to display a theme line — themes are always good marketing
- when you have made a few sales of higher priced items, you can display images of the sold pieces to help establish a confidence factor; that your work is worth what you say it is
- maintain an 'About me' area where you can post your bio, list your education, grants, awards, testimonies and published articles and reviews

Auction listing fees are slightly lower for eBay stores. Art and craft sellers report having a store seems to support their individual auction listings and vice versa.

For promoting your eBay store elsewhere, you'll get a URL like: http://ebaystores.com/yourstorename

eBay Keyword program

For more experienced sellers, eBay's Keyword program allows Sellers with an eBay store or item currently for sale to select specific words and phrases as their keywords.

When users type these keywords into the eBay Search box, a customized banner ad that matches the searchers keywords to your product will be displayed above the normal listing results for their search.

What happens if ten people want the same keywords? You bid how much you'll pay for an actual click on your banner. The highest bid takes the number one position. With a limited number of 'slots' available to banners, the higher bids will get higher priority on those slots and higher frequency.

The minimum bid is $.10 per click. For popular keywords, expect higher pay-per-click bidding.

Selecting two and three word phrases will get you more qualified buyers than selecting individual keywords that are very broad. For instance, 'stained glass angels' will get you more targeted bidders than 'angels'.

Understand that you are paying for each click on a banner ad, regardless of whether the visitor actually bids on your item. Also know that people realize they are looking at an ad, no matter how fancy the banner, so their defenses are automatically raised.

If you choose to get involved in the Keywords program, you should test the effectiveness of banner ads for each item before committing to any long term strategy. If you see improved sales and profits, then you can gradually roll out more ads, continuing to test and measure their effectiveness.

Before you get involved with the eBay Keyword program, know your market and have plenty of successful auctions behind you so you can accurately forecast how much of your profit margin you can afford to allocate to pay-per-click banners. For more details, see www.ebaykeywords.com

Become a Power Seller

eBay Power Sellers get extra perks because they have achieved high standards while running their eBay business. Power Sellers have a 98% feedback rating and good sales performance record. To become a Power Seller, just apply when you feel your ready.

One of the benefits of becoming a Power Seller is access to priority customer support and technical assistance for your eBay accounts. Power Sellers enjoy exclusive offers like eBay co-op advertising, which means getting reimbursement for your advertising efforts. Power Sellers get up to $200 in banner ads per quarter. You may even qualify for a healthcare plan. Additional perks include exclusive offerings, 'best practices' discussion board and invitations to special events. For more information on becoming a Power Seller, see http://pages.ebay.com/services/buyandsell/powerseller/criteria.html

Chapter 11
Order Fulfillment

This chapter helps you deal with the process of sending orders to winning auction bidders in ways that cut your costs, protect you from future complications before they happen, and turn onetime buyers into lifetime customers.

Packaging

Whatever you sell, the item will require some form of packaging before shipping to the customer. Books and tools can get scratched or their sharp edges can cut through a mailing envelope. Use extra cardboard or bubble wrap to prevent damage to the mailing package itself.

Fragile items like pottery or glass will require extra bubble wrap or paper to cushion objects during transit. You don't want to get stuck with paying for items broken in shipping.

Locate supplies of shipping boxes, padded mailers, bubble wrap and other packaging supplies by searching for "shipping supplies" on eBay and on Google. I've found Associated Bag Company to be low in prices with excellent service; see www.associatedbag.com

The U.S. Postal Service will supply you with free Priority Mail boxes, labels and packing tape. Just ask at your local post office for the number to call or visit www.usps.com.

Shipping

In most mail order transactions, the buyer pays for shipping. The same is generally true for auction purchases. If you scan several auction listings at eBay, you will find a variety of seller shipping and handling charges.

Some sellers try to raise their profits by adding on handling charges and exaggerating the shipping amount. Auction shoppers are sharp enough to recognize inflated shipping costs. I had a bad experience buying software once where the seller charged me $10 to ship a CD via Priority Mail, which only cost him $4. I'll never buy from him again.

For heavier items, you won't always know the exact amount of shipping because rates vary according to the recipient's address. What you can do is include a statement on your auction description saying something like "Once I know your shipping address, your exact shipping costs will be given at auction's end". eBay's Shipping Center links to USPS and UPS to calculate shipping costs, print labels and track packages.

Some buyers will be leery of bidding on items where no shipping costs are stated. Adding a statement like the one above will help instill confidence in bidders.

Also include a statement of the means by which you ship — UPS, USPS, FedEx or any other shippers. No one shipper is going to always be the cheapest for all of your products if you sell a variety of items. When you make notes of your package weights and the shipping costs via the different services, you'll soon know which company is cheapest for a given package.

If you sell and ship books, audio cassettes, VHS tapes and computer media like CDs and DVDs, you can save money on shipping costs by sending these items "Media Rate" which is much cheaper than First Class or Priority Mail. Media Rate takes 7 to 10 days and cannot contain any advertisements. An online service providing postage, labels and Delivery Confirmation for media and other rates of postage is www.endicia.com.

Offer free shipping

Another approach is to include shipping charges in the amount you set as the opening bid price for the item and offer free shipping. Put the words **"Free Shipping"** in bold letters on your auction description and you will get more bids. A recent survey showed online buyers want free shipping above other perks.

Try different methods and track the results. For instance, if you see a measurable increase in sales after you have included free shipping, you know that's a profitable approach.

Consider adding a statement on your item description that the buyer will save on shipping costs of several items if they win more than one auction. Remember that auction bidders are looking for the best deal or they wouldn't be bidding.

Delivery confirmation

Always ship with some form of delivery confirmation. Otherwise, you have no means of proof that the customer received a shipment should they claim they had not.

UPS and FedEx have delivery confirmation built into their rates. If shipping via USPS Priority Mail, you can get free delivery confirmation by using 'Click N Ship' online at www.usps.com or through your Pay Pal account. 'Click N Ship' allows you to print your own labels. You pay extra fees for delivery confirmation when mailing and paying from a physical post office.

If you plan to sell and ship internationally, don't ever ship overseas without some form of delivery confirmation by signature. The cheapest way I've found is to insure the shipment which requires a signature upon delivery. Or you can also send the item by register mail overseas.

People in other countries have bought items which I shipped off without having them sign for delivery. Then three months later, they claimed to have never received the items, which led to a merchant charge back on my credit card merchant account. When you get too many chargebacks within a short period, the merchant account provider puts your company name on a blacklist and it's very difficult to get a merchant account again. Although I managed to avoid the black-list, I ended up losing $700 from overseas shipments before instigating signed delivery requirements.

Insurance

Most items have the possibility of damage during shipping, especially handmade pieces. Although you can and should do everything you can to protect items being shipped with adequate packaging, you can't prevent a hurried driver from throwing your package around. I've painfully observed postal clerks toss my package right in front of my eyes as if to show me they don't much care what happens to it.

There's may be customers who get an item, decide they don't like it, and claim it arrived damaged during shipment. UPS and FedEx include up to $100 insurance per package in their shipping rates. If you ship by postal mail, insurance is an extra charge.

Consider offering an additional charge for insurance on all items. Suppose you offer your customer an option of paying $1 for extra insurance. If your products are not easily damaged in shipping, you could earn extra money from those who elect to pay the insurance charge. The money would go into your own "self-insurance" fund. Depending on your items and your carrier, you may have more money coming into the fund than going out to pay actual insurance costs.

Order fulfillment

After you've been notified your auction has closed with a winning bidder, contact the winner immediately and arrange for payment. According to eBay's guidelines, you should ship the item within three days of receiving payment. It's always good for customer relations to ship orders right away. Send email to the buyer to let them know their item has shipped.

When you are prompt, professional and polite you'll get a happy, satisfied customer who will leave you good feedback and be open to future offers.

Make a point to send a 'Thank You' email and about a week later, a follow-up email checking to see if the customer got their order.

Customer list

Selling your art and craft items on eBay through auctions allows you to gather complete contact information of buyers and eBay "handles" of bidders. A "handle" is the nickname you use as a registered eBay user.

Store this information in a database or spreadsheet program that allows you to organize, sort, and create labels easily.

You will especially want to be able to sort out email addresses, since email costs you nothing to send. Although mass emailing your prospects is a bad policy, set up a system of follow-up with personalized emails to build good customer relationships.

Create a set of standard or canned email replies ready for commonly asked questions such as item details, care instructions, and exactly what the customer must expect to do if he wins the auction. Yes, people will ask you for information that is clearly available on your pages and you should respond politely sending them that same information.

Customer retention

You may think former customers will naturally want to contact you the next time they are ready to buy. But the truth is people may never think of you after your first sale unless you have put your name in front of them enough times that your name rises to the top of their thoughts when they need an art or craft item.

One survey showed 68% of customers saying the reason they did not return to do business with a merchant because they were treated with indifference by an employee or owner.

In general, 80% of your business will come from 20% of your customers. People who buy art and craft items often do so as collectors. It makes good marketing sense for you to cultivate long-term relationships with buyers. The successful artist will always strive to create relationships knowing that a customer will have a lifetime value which far exceeds a one-time sale.

Newsletter

Since people took the time to place a bid for one of your items, you know they have an interest. You can easily create a newsletter with periodic announcements from you about new items, closeouts and special sales which customers and prospects can get by email or at your Web site.

Create a PDF file One-Page Newsletter to either send as an email attachment or make available as a Web site download. According to Roger C. Parker, author of 35 books including *The Streetwise Guide to Relationship Marketing on the Internet,* One-Page Newsletters make it easy to keep in constant touch with past customers — traditionally your most profitable source of new business.

It costs seven times as much to attract and sell a new customer than it does to contact and resell a past customer.

One-Page Newsletters are monthly, educationally focused, carefully formatted publications that appear on both sides of a single sheet of paper. They are primarily intended for free monthly email and web site distribution. Copies can, however, be printed as needed on desktop printers for handout and mailings.

The one-page format is long enough to communicate a compelling story, yet short enough to be efficiently produced each month.

The more time that goes by between customer contacts, the less chance you have of making additional sales. Being visible to your customers each month ensures that you will never be forgotten, that you will enjoy "top of mind" awareness when it's time for your auction buyers and prospects to buy.

If you need help formatting a newsletter, see Roger's free samples and articles at onepagenewsletters.com. Download his free "Secrets of the One-Page Newsletter."

Contacting bidders on eBay

Although the seller doesn't have access to the direct email of all bidders, he can contact bidders through their handle name, but he has to be careful to do so in ways that are not against eBay's policies. Here's what they say about contacting other users:

> To better protect the privacy of eBay users, you can only request contact information for eBay users who are involved in your current or recent transactions. Examples are:
> • Sellers can request contact information for all buyers in an active listing and the winning buyer in successful, closed listings.
> • Buyers can request contact information for a seller during an ongoing listing and in a successful, closed listing if they are the winning bidder or buyer.

and in their User Agreement:

> By entering into our User Agreement, you agree that, with respect to other users' personal information that you obtain through the Site or through an eBay-related communication or eBay-facilitated transaction, eBay hereby grants to you a license to use such information only for: (a) eBay-related communications that are not unsolicited commercial messages, (b) using services offered through eBay (e.g. escrow, insurance, shipping and fraud complaints), and (c) any other purpose that a user expressly agrees to after you tell them the purpose you would like to use it for. In all cases, you must give users an opportunity to remove themselves from your database and a chance to review what information you have collected about them. In addition, under no circumstances, except as defined in this Section, can you disclose personal information about another user to any third party without our consent and the consent of that user.

You can send a note through a bidder's handle to mention details about an auction. You can then ask permission to send them information about your newsletter.

Another way to let bidders know you have a newsletter is to announce it on each auction description page.

Use your 'About Me' page to let bidders know about the newsletter, though not all bidders will visit that page.

Yet another place to put a note about a newsletter is when you make use of eBay's "Second Chance Offer" described below.

A good reason to create a mailing list of your prospects is that if something unforeseen happens to eBay and their site becomes unavailable or eBay changes such that you do not choose to work with them, you still have your customer list.

Second chance to buy

eBay has set up a way to give losing bidders another opportunity to get the item they wanted through a feature called "Second Chance Offer". On these sales, eBay doesn't charge insertion fees but after your item sells, eBay will charge you the applicable final value fees.

"Second Chance Offer" items are only accessible to you and your unsuccessful bidders and can be initiated from the completed auction page. See http://pages.ebay.com//help/sellerguide/faq-personaloffer.html.

Excuses to follow-up

In addition to contacting bidders who did not win with a second chance offer, there are many more excellent reasons to follow-up with customers and bidders. Here are 22:

- to thank your customer after the sale
- to thank bidders for their interest even if they lost
- to let bidders know about a similar offer
- to announce a special sale to past bidders
- to announce a contest

- to announce a new product through your eBay store
- to announce a limited edition series
- to send a product sample
- to advise about discontinued items
- to learn if a customer got their order
- to send a newsletter
- to send a postcard or flyer with schedule of your shows and exhibits
- to send educational articles which explain more about your art or craft
- to ask for a referral
- to invite people when you are teaching a class in their area or at a national event
- to thank someone for a referral
- to express the pleasure of working with someone
- to offer a coupon
- to make your customer feel important by creating a preferred customer offering
- to send interesting facts about the item a customer bought
- to send a customer survey asking for feedback on how you measured up for service and quality of product
- to resolve a conflict or problem the customer had

Two free email management programs for working with large groups of email addresses are Eudora at www.eudora.com and Pegasus at www.pmail.com.

Chapter 12
How to Fine Tune
Your Auction Success

Bulk listing tools

Let's say you've put up a few auctions, made a little money and now you're ready to roll out more listings. You certainly don't want to spend hours and hours listing multiple auctions one at a time. The solution is to use an bulk listing tool, like *Turbo Lister.*

Turbo Lister is a free desktop software tool available on eBay designed to make listing multiple items faster and easier. *Turbo Lister* lets you list multiple items all at once and save listings to re-use again and again. The tool also lets you build your auction pages with HTML templates. Schedule the times you want your auctions to begin and end. To download *Turbo Lister*, go to http://pages.ebay.com/turbo_lister/

There are more sophisticated software seller tools available through eBay at various fees. As your auction business grows, your need for organizing and posting multiple auctions may suggest more advanced tools. Do a search for 'auction seller tool" at www.google.com and you'll get a huge list. But don't spend the money on any tool unless the use of it will result in increased revenues.

Your 'About Me' page

Create an 'About Me' page to help buyers know who you are. Telling your story will help instill customer confidence by giving bidders a connection with a live person. Craft sellers should include a photo of themselves to help establish credibility. Also, consider creating a logo to include in all of your listings. A logo will help buyers recognize your eBay brand and is something you can use off the Web in your promotional materials, too.

Buyers of art and craft like to know about the artist. Your *About Me* page should include your bio, awards, education, testimonials, grants, articles and media interviews.

Create a long version of about three to four paragraphs and a short version of a single paragraph. When promoting your name online or offline, you'll find occasions to need a choice of bio length. I also recommend you create a 7-word blurb that tells what's unique about your work.

If you haven't received kudos and accolades yet, start collecting them. You'll need them for promoting your art or craft no matter where you sell.

More auction tips

• When choosing your user name on eBay, keep your choice short, catchy and memorable. Try to get a name which might relate to your media, like 'photoluv' or 'beadqueen'. Avoid creating a user name which may inadvertently offend prospective buyers. For example, you would not want to choose a user name that showed you were either a Democrat or a Republican, because whichever party you affiliate with, your name will offend most everyone else in the other party.

• Try listing your items as regular auctions and Dutch auctions to see which type of auction produces more sales and higher profits. Dutch auctions allow you to sell multiple quantities of an item through a single auction listing.

• When composing your auction listing, include extensive details describing your item. You don't have to worry about space because there is plenty. People cannot know anything about what you are selling other than the words and photos you provide. However, avoid using advertising words like 'most beautiful', 'best available' or 'this is the greatest'. Instead give them bulleted details which allow them to draw their own conclusions about how great your item is.

- Avoid saying you are a new artist, even if you are. Write with confidence, because people buy confidence.
- Keep your auction page layout clean (not necessarily short) and to the point. Avoid including fancy borders and non-relevant graphics just because you can. The most popular page on the Internet is Google.com's home page. Notice how refreshingly simple it is.
- Don't close your auction down early just because there are no bids. Many bidders wait until the last minute to bid.
- Clearly state your terms, that is, what bidders have to do if they win the auction. Be sure to name all and everything that will cost money, like shipping and insurance fees, if any.
- Make your emails to customers friendly and it will help you create a loyal following. A friend of mine who sells via auctions as a full time business reports that, because he has personalized his email responses to bidders, he has built up a regular base of customers who email him regularly with requests for new offers.
- Mail invitations to your auctions to your existing customers by email or post cards. Offer free shipping, discount coupons off future auctions or purchases from your Web site, free promotional giveaways or any other promotional offer that would motivate visitors to check out your auctions or your Web site.

Create backups

The more you get involved with selling on eBay, the more product description files, canned emails, customer lists, supplier information, and images you will accumulate. To protect your investment and provide for fast recovery in the event of a catastrophic computer failure, create a system for backing up your files.

Make file folders on your computer directory's hard drive which clearly tell you what you are storing. Name directories simply like 'Images' and 'Descriptions'.

However you organize your data files, store them in a separate directory from your program application files. Doing so will facilitate your backup and recovery procedures and make the files easier to access.

How to stay current with eBay changes

eBay is constantly evolving, just as the way people use the Web evolves. If you are intent on building a successful eBay business, you must keep up to date.

One of the best ways to learn about changes eBay makes is through your notification preferences. Go to http://pages.ebay.com/services/myebay/optin-login.html, log in to your account and select the notifications you will allow eBay to send you. You can choose to get email notices of your item's bid status, listing confirmations, invoices, updates to policies and special offers from eBay.

To get specific help on selling art and craft items and learn about changes on eBay, visit eBay's own forum for craft sellers at http://forums.ebay.com/db2/forum.jsp?forum=27. You can read what other sellers say about important issues and updates and post comments. Plus you can ask questions from other users.

When you first begin participating on eBay's or any other forum, browse previous postings before jumping in with a question. There's a good chance other newbies have asked similar questions you have and already posted answers you can read there.

Outside of eBay, there are many sites with resources for auction sellers:

• www.thebidfloor.com/forms.htm - amazing collection of free forms and links to resources for conducting a successful auction business.

• www.auctionbytes.com/Email_Newsletter/calendar/calendar.html - lets you know which day of the month is statistically better for beginning your auction.

• www.AuctionMole.com - provides the following free

tools for running online auction business. At their site you will find:

> *Auction Digger* is designed to scan multiple auction sites for phrases you submit. It will then report pricing and sales statistics for auctions that contain your search phrase.
>
> *eBay Fee Calculator* lets you calculate what your total costs will be for a particular auction on eBay. Know ahead of time just what you're getting into.
>
> *Hot Spotter* allows you to get "Hot Item" reports from one or more eBay auction categories and subcategories.

For more help, see eBay's *Craft Sellers Guide,* at http://pages.ebay.com/CraftsSellerGuide/ From this guide, eBay offers a convenient search page to locate trading assistants appropriate for art and craft items. You can also search eBay's list of auction tools.

Chapter 13
More Income Streams from eBay

Sell art and craft supplies

In Chapter 2, you will find examples of successfully completed items listed by search terms. As mentioned, not all the listings analyzed are for finished handmade art or craft items. Many of the same words you use to describe your work will be used by sellers who offer popular art, craft and framing supplies, which are in growing demand on eBay.

Selling art and craft supplies is a great way to lower your own production costs while bringing in added revenue. It is easy to sell your excess art, craft and photography supplies, books, magazines, newsletters, tools and equipment on eBay.

I'm the first to acknowledge that a business selling art or craft supplies is a leap away from creating beautiful one-of-a-kind items. However, I also think creating multiple income streams is smart business.

If you can lower the material costs of the items you make now by buying your supplies in bulk directly from manufacturers instead of retailers, your profit margin will immediately and significantly increase. For more ways of locating wholesale sources, see Chapter 3.

The catch is that buying in bulk often means buying in larger quantities, probably much more than you need at any given time in producing your art or craft. A profitable solution is to sell your excess craft supplies on eBay. Offline, you can also sell supplies retail by mail by placing ads in craft magazines.

In order to cut the costs of producing my handwoven garments, I began ordering yarns direct from yarn mills instead of buying through retailers.

The mills typically wanted orders of $250 and more and
n the yarns were closeouts. However, the prices were
much less than I had been paying. For example, for some
cotton yarns which I previously paid $6 per pound through a
retail yarn supplier, I could get through the mills for less than
$1 a pound.

I began running ads in the weaving magazines, asking $3
for a set of samples. My ad described the yarns as closeouts
and noted that dye lots could not be guaranteed to match.

I marked up the $1 per pound yarns to $4 a pound and
brought in more money than it cost to run the ads and make
up the samples. It was a bargain for my customers and I made
money as well as lowered my production material costs.

You can add another income stream to this business idea
by teaching classes in your chosen media. You'll make money
from teaching and have new customers who will buy their
craft supplies from you. You can teach classes in your craft at
adult education venues and college continuing education
programs or even at your own studio. You will get paid for
teaching and you will make money selling the supplies at
retail.

Okay, since we're on a roll here, how about writing a
book about your expertise and add yet another income stream.
You can advertise your craft supplies in the back of the book.
Of course, your students will buy your books, as will craft
supply stores. Worried about finding a publisher? Technology
is on the side of the self-publisher. You can now print as few
books as you need without investing thousands of dollars in
inventory. See www.00ebooks.com for more ideas.

eBay Trading Assistants

You can hire an experienced eBay seller to list your and
sell your items for you. Trading Assistants (TAs) will charge
you fees in addition to eBay's auction listing fees.

I found 21 eBay TAs from all around the U.S. listed with
experience in selling craft items. Their fees ranged anywhere

from 5% to 30% of the sale plus all applicable eBay fees. Because you will pay commissions to TAs, make sure you know your costs and profit margins to insure you make back your inventory expenses and some profit for yourself.

When you've gained experience selling through your own auctions, you can apply to become a TA yourself. Once you get listed in the Trading Assistants directory, you are announcing that you are willing to sell for others. Since you can charge fees for your services as a TA, this is an added revenue stream for you.

Selling as a TA allows you to leverage your selling expertise without having to find product yourself. Clients whom you sell for provide the items and you get paid for your efforts on terms that you decide. Many sellers already do this as a way of making money on eBay and profit margins can be lucrative for high-priced items.

You can find out more about how to locate or become a Trading Assistant on eBay's craft seller guide at http:// pages.ebay.com/CraftsSellerGuide/

Earn money from eBay's affiliate program

Even if you don't have a product to sell on eBay, you can earn money as an affiliate. An affiliate is an independent contractor who agrees to send traffic to a merchant who sells a product or service and pays the affiliate a commission of each sale. Simply put, affiliates earn money for referring business.

By sending traffic to eBay through affiliate coded links on your site, you get paid when those visitors place a bid for an auction or sign up as a new user. eBay pays .05 cents per bid and $5 for every new user. The commission rates go up for higher volume referrers.

eBay developed a sophisticated affiliate tool called the *eBay Editor Kit* that allows you to build highly targeted interactive graphic banners which list specific items for sale on eBay.

For instance, if you were an affiliate wishing to promote

ribbons, you can quickly build a graphic box to place on your site that shows only auctions for ribbons. The more targeted your site traffic, the more likely people will click-through to specific auctions. As an example, see www.craft-supplies-usa.com/dream-catcher-craft-supplies.htm for how I promote dream catcher supplies.

Since using the *eBay Editor Kit* and placing graphics displaying targeted auctions, my recorded click-through rate has averaged between 50% and 70%. This compares to a typical click-through rate on my other affiliate links of between 2% to 15%.

To become an affiliate for eBay, your web site must be approved. Your site must get steady traffic, look good and all the links should function. Typically, eBay is interested in well-designed, high traffic sites to partner with. To apply, sign up at www.cj.com, Commission Junction.

> NOTE: It is against eBay's affiliate policies for you to use *eBay Editor Kit* to link to your own eBay auctions.

Listing your eBay auctions in more places

You can list your eBay auctions at other sites on the Web by posting on discussion groups which allow craft sales listings: http://groups.yahoo.com/group/crafts/ is a group specifically for selling arts and crafts.

You can locate more discussion groups at http://groups.msn.com or http://groups.google.com. However, be sure to read each group's rules about posting. Only groups that say it's okay to list ads will accept your auction listings.

It is possible your eBay auction listing mentioned in discussion groups may show up in search engine results queries, depending on how well you include popular search terms used to describe your auctions.

Chapter 14
How to Track and Measure Results

It is important that you stay on top of how your efforts, time and money spent on auctions yields profits. A successful auction seller keeps track of her business using simple systems to record data from sales, expenses, suppliers, and elements included in her auction listings.

Many of the auction management software programs allow you to record and analyze your own auctions. Just do a search for "auction management" on eBay or Google to review the many options.

Spreadsheets or databases are also easy for organizing, sorting and printing auction data. Most spreadsheet programs let you view records as graphs, which is very helpful when looking for trends and cycles.

Sales are easy to track. Just count up the number of sales that come through every day. Divide the total of your sales dollars by the number of completed auctions for the same period to learn the average dollar value of each auction.

By recording and measuring your sales and other variables like category choices and feature upgrades, you are able to observe growth over time and assess the efficiency of your efforts.

It's fairly simple to know what to do when you know what's happening in your business. When you don't know what's happening, your decisions will be based on memory and guesswork, which are okay in the beginning. But as you add more and more auctions and ship more and more orders, you're going to need the ability to quickly analyze weeks and months of recorded details in order to know where you are losing money and where you stand to gain more profits.

Although it may seem obvious, it is also easy to forget that it pays you to remember you will want to do more auctions that are successful and drop ones which aren't. Likewise, you want to move toward higher closing prices for your auctions and consistently look for ways to lower your costs.

You can only know what to do when you can measure these items that affect your bottom line:

• Sales — Record your total sales and sales according to category. This is the way to learn that some categories might be more profitable than others. You may discover listings under one category gets more number of sales, while another category results in higher closing bids.

• Cost of sales ratio — Calculate the total amount of eBay's seller fees to see what percentage of the sale amount is a selling cost.

• Conversion rate — How many of your auction listings complete successfully? What can you do to improve the number of successful closings?

• Average selling price — This is the total amount of item sales divided by the number of completed auctions. I showed you earlier how to find the average selling prices of items like yours. You should also track your own average selling prices over time so you can project a predictable profit margin and learn how much money you have available for experimenting with ideas for boosting sales

• Cost of goods — Record your total costs for each item and consistently look for cheaper suppliers to lower the cost of items you sell.

Using counters

By using a counter such as those available widely on the Web or from Andale.com, you can track the number of times your auction listings get viewed. Although this may be satisfying on some level, the only real measure of your auction success is getting bidders who bid your price up to a profitable closing. Counters do, however, allow you to track the effectiveness of upgrade features like Gallery or Featured by telling you how many visitors actually viewed auction pages which include those upgrades.

Not so final note . . .

In closing, keep a couple of key points in mind for selling your craft items on eBay and you'll do great.

√ Always do your research before placing a listing

√ Don't violate eBay's policies

√ Consistently look for lower priced items to sell

√ Join eBay's forums to learn how others sell

√ Keep this book close at hand — it's a blueprint for your success on eBay.

Bonus Gifts

Here are the 3 bonuses that accompany your ebook:

(1) <u>Deep Analysis</u> is powerful software that can analyze the art and craft eBay market sector and produce detailed market research reports. Analyze a particular craft item to see how much it might sell for, and find the best techniques for selling it. See which craft sellers are really doing well, and analyze their techniques and product line. Find out how much your competitors are really selling in your marketplace. Strategize which categories would be best for your art and craft items by viewing bid data, sell-through rates, and average sales. Boost your craft sales by knowing which items receive the most bids and which sell for the most. For your free 30-day trial, go to **www.craftmarketer.com/ebay_auction_software_tools.htm**

(2) <u>WhizAnalysis</u> Provides precise sales analysis and statistics for the eBay crafts market. Points out the potential art and craft items that can make money based on the most accurate statistics. Offers craft sellers a personalized performance and pricing report on each item. Indicates all items that are "Making Money Currently". Identifies which seller is making money presently. Provides chart analysis which offer the broadest picture of the eBay market. For your free 30-day trial, go to **www.craftmarketer.com/ebay_auction_software_tools.htm**

(3) *Make Your Auction Sell: Masters Course* (PDF ebook in ZIP format, apx. 1.7MB) The approach is unique and powerful — you will not read this in any other auction book, at any price, anywhere on or off the Net. Sydney Johnston, a well-respected expert in the Net auction world (who literally makes

hundreds of thousands of dollars through online auctions), gives you the benefit of all her knowledge and experience in "Make Your Net Auction Sell!, The Masters Course."

She helps you get started the right way. She takes you step by step through the process. You'll avoid the pitfalls and innocent mistakes due to inexperience. And most importantly of all . . you will generate great income and build a business that you own (instead of being dependent upon eBay) — you know, the enough-to-save-for-retirement type of income. To download your free *Make Your Net Auction Sell!, The Masters Course*, go to **www.craftmarketer.com/ ebay_auction_software_tools.htm**

About the Author

    James Dillehay, author of nine books, is a nationally recognized expert on marketing art and craft. With over 19 years experience as an artist, entrepreneur, and educator, his articles have helped over 15,000,000 readers of *Family Circle, The Crafts Report, Better Homes & Gardens: Crafting for Profit, Sunshine Artist, Ceramics Monthly, Florida Retirement Lifestyles* and more. His books are recommended by many of the major craft magazines and on HGTV. James serves as a member of the advisory boards to the National Craft Association and ArtisanStreet.com.

    James answers marketing questions from business owners on Jay Conrad Levinson's Guerrilla Marketing Association forum and at AllExperts.com where he is consistently rated a top expert. He advises artists and craftspeople on Craftmarketer.com, the most popular Web site online for learning the business of selling crafts.

Guerrilla Marketing for Artists & Craftspeople by Jay Conrad Levinson and James Dillehay

Get over 100 Guerrilla Marketing tactics specifically for artists and craftspeople. Learn how to make your work stand out. Discover the 7 Step Marketing Plan for artisans. Explore a myriad of overlooked markets for art, craft and design. Read stories about artists and craftspeople who used imaginative marketing methods to become wildly successful, like the two hippies who turned their art and poetry into a multimillion dollar empire and a bankrupt artist who went on to create a billion dollar industry. Learn step-by-step how to create your own Guerrilla Marketing calendar using scores of low-cost and free promotional tactics.

Jay Conrad Levinson is author of the Guerrilla Marketing series of books, Over 14 million sold; now in 39 languages. James Dillehay is a nationally recognized expert in marketing art and crafts.

Guerrilla Marketing for Artists & Craftspeople is due in July 2004. To order, see www.craftmarketer.com/guerrilla-marketing.htm

The Basic Guide to Selling Arts & Crafts by James Dillehay. Gives step-by-step help on over 150 topics. Find the best fairs, sell to stores, get interior designers and corporations to buy your work, make money from spin-off ideas, sell your crafts mail order, discover overlooked markets, what to do when your work isn't selling. Appendixes list over 250 sources and reference books for the artisan. Selected as the official text of the American Professional Crafter's Guild. Reviewed on Amazon.com as *"the how-to of how-to books."* 189 pages, illustrations. Item #100 $14.95 for softcover

The Basic Guide to Pricing Your Craftwork by James Dillehay. One of the most often asked questions from craftpersons selling their work is *"How much should I charge?"* Whether you are a seasoned professional or just starting, this guide will give you the tools to become more profitable and competitive. You will learn basic formulas for pricing your craftwork in selling retail or wholesale, how to use pricing strategies to increase sales, how to increase the perceived value of your products, how to know if you are really making a profit, how to keep records, and how to manage your time and workspace to reduce your labor costs and boost productivity. You also get examples of many tax advantages from your craft business. Your success as a professional crafter may very well depend on what you find in this guide. 139 pages, illustrated, charts, index. Item #400 $12.95 for softcover edition

The Basic Guide to Selling Crafts On the Internet by James Dillehay. Discover how the Internet can help you sell more of your craftwork and lower your marketing costs. Includes using a web site, search engines, email, discussion groups, online auctions, publicity, advertising and hundreds of more tips. (Note: This book includes a chapter on auction tips, but if you are only interested in selling on eBay, get ***Sell Your Crafts on eBay*** for much more detailed help with auctions.) Learn which keywords to include in your site content in order to capture free traffic from the search engines. Appendixes list resources including sites to get free graphics and software, free web pages, free tutorials on web design for business, online media contacts, free newsletters and newsgroups about your craft and internet marketing. Indexed, illustrated, 168 pages. Item #102 $16.95 softcover edition

Directory of Grants for Crafts and How to Write a Winning Proposal by James Dillehay. Learn everything you need to know about locating and getting free money through grants from foundations, corporations and the government. Learn how to draft a grant proposal and fill in grant applications. Learn how to follow the grant process from planning to submitting. This guide includes over 1,000 listings, contact information and subject areas of grants available for artists and crafts persons. 216 pages, Item #101 $19.95 for the softcover edition

Your Guide to Ebook Publishing Success by James Dillehay. Whether you are a writer seeking ways to bypass the frustrations and delays of dealing with getting published or a self-publisher looking to take advantage of the latest ebook marketing strategies, this book provides step-by-step help for profiting from digital publishing. This is a do-it-yourself manual written for those who want to keep control of how their material is produced and marketed. Use the tactics described to become a completely, self-sufficient publisher, distributor and bookseller. 170 pages, 6" x 9", softcover, illustrated, $16.95

Order these books and more at **www.Craftmarketer.com** and sign up for the *Craftmarketer Newsletter* to get tips and news about marketing arts and crafts.

Printed in the United States
22462LVS00003B/58

9 780971 068452